Guan Yin
The Buddha's Helper

Retold from the Lotus Sutra

written by Bhikshuni Jin Rou and Terri Nicholson
illustrated by Bhikshuni Heng Ching

Instilling Goodness Books
An imprint of Buddhist Text Translation Society, Ukiah, CA

Guan Yin
The Buddha's Helper

Retold from the Lotus Sutra

Written by Bhikshuni Jin Rou and Terri Nicholson
Illustrated by Bhikshuni Heng Ching
Book design by Amandine DAM–Levendivin

Based on the *Wonderful Dharma Lotus Flower Sutra*, translated and published by Buddhist Text Translation Society

Published by Instilling Goodness Books
imprint of Buddhist Text Translation Society
4951 Bodhi Way, Ukiah, CA 95482

www.buddhisttexts.org

Buddhist Text Translation Society
4951 Bodhi Way, Ukiah, CA 95482
www.buddhisttexts.org
info@buddhisttexts.org

ISBN 978-1-64217-021-4 (hardcover)

Cataloging in Publication Data is available from the Library of Congress.

Guan Yin is the Buddha's helper. She is kind and wise and helps all the beings on earth. Helping is her job. When someone needs help, she can appear in any form to help them, but she never tells anyone who she is.

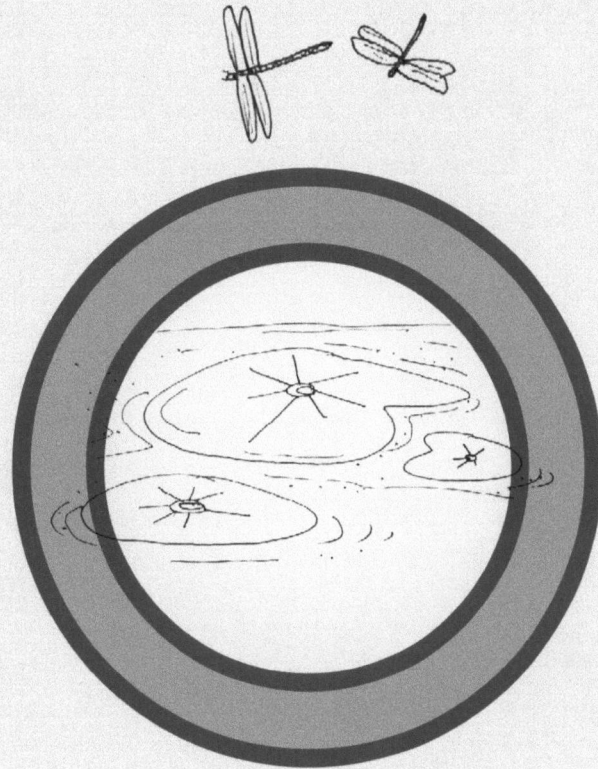

People from different places make statues and paintings of Guan Yin. The statues and paintings are as different as the artists who create them, so are her names.

In China, she is called Guan Yin. She sprinkles sweet dew from her vase, washing our troubles away and making us happy.

In Vietnam, she is called Quan Am. She stands on the head of a dragon and saves ships at sea.

In Korea, she is called Guan Im. She heals illness with her willow branch and gladdens the hearts of all.

In India and Tibet, she is called Avalokiteśvara
(Ah-vah-lo-kee-tesh-vah-rah).
She has a thousand hands with a thousand eyes to
reach out to all beings.

In Japan, she is called Kannon. She protects children and animals with her loving-kindness.

In America, she is called the Bodhisattva (Boh-dee-saht-vah) of Great Compassion. She radiates peace and harmony in the world.

If you need Guan Yin's help, recite her name with all your heart. She will be there.

Namo Guan Shr Yin Pusa
Namo Guan Shr Yin Pusa
Namo Guan Shr Yin Pusa

Namo means to show respect by putting your palms together.

Guan Shr Yin means to listen to the sounds of the world.

Pusa means Bodhisattva. Bodhisattvas wish for everyone to become like Buddhas, kind, wise and compassionate. Guan Yin is the Bodhisattva of Great Compassion.

If you're afraid of spiders and creepy, crawly things, recite Guan Yin's name. She'll help you to be brave and kind to them.

If you are sick or hurt, recite Guan Yin's name with all your heart and you will feel better.

When the lights go out and you think you
hear a monster, recite Guan Yin's name and
you will feel safe.

If you feel sad or lonely, recite Guan Yin's name. And like a moon reflected in water, you will feel happy and peaceful again.

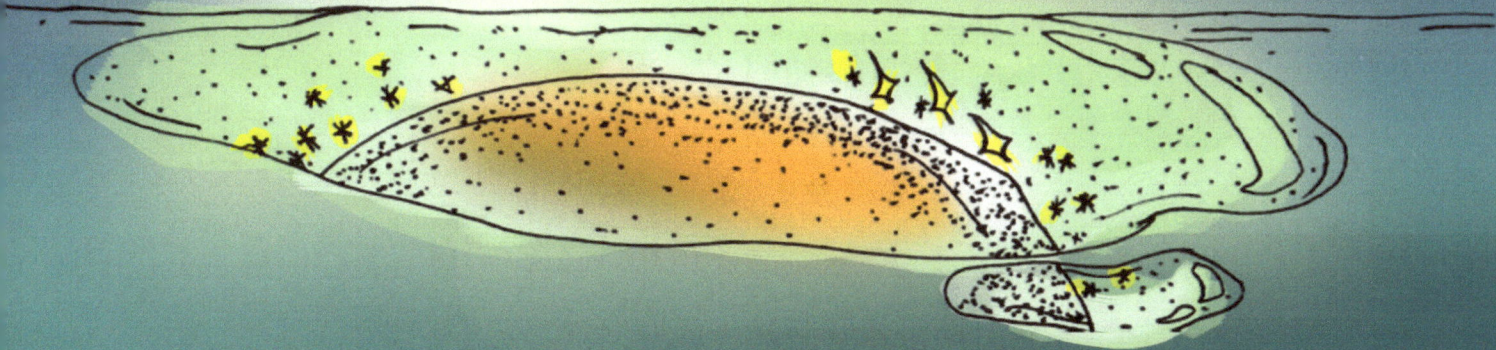

If you're having trouble with
friends, recite Guan Yin's name

and think it over. Try using kind words and give them the help they need.

If you have a big temper, recite Guan Yin's name and reset your mind. Your anger will settle down like gentle waves on the sea.

If you have a problem studying,
recite Guan Yin's name. You can then focus on
your lessons and not think of other things.

If someone you love dies, recite Guan Yin's name. She will comfort you and help you remember the good times you had together.

If you want something you can't have, recite Guan Yin's name and you can be happy even without it.

If you make a mistake, recite Guan Yin's name and you'll feel better. Making mistakes is how we learn and grow.

Guan Yin is always there like the part inside you that is wise and kind. All you have to do is recite her name. The more you recite, the more she will help you. She's a good friend to have around.

Namo Guan Shr Yin Bodhisattva
Namo Guan Shr Yin Bodhisattva
Namo Guan Shr Yin Bodhisattva

Instilling Goodness Books

The Kind Monk

The Buddha's Helper

Snow-Covered Peaks

No Words—Teachings of the Buddha

The Giant King Turtle (English, Chinese & Spanish)

The Legend of Mahadutta (English & Spanish)

The Awakened One (English & Chinese)

The Light of Hope (English & Chinese)

Under the Bodhi Tree

Come Back, O Tiger!

Instilling Goodness Books is a branch of the Buddhist Text Translation Society. Its goal is to open the hearts and minds of children to their full potential through art and story. Ancient Buddhist stories are retold in their language on how to be wise, kind and thoughtful to beings of all kinds. The center is located at the City of Ten Thousand Buddhas in Ukiah Valley, California, a spiritual community founded by Venerable Master Husan Hua. It is the home of Dharma Realm Buddhist University and Instilling Goodness Elementary School and Developing Virtue Secondary School.

The schools offer a unique educational program that goes beyond the state requirements and focuses on developing qualities such as filial respect, compassion, and integrity.

Meditation and bilingual education in English and Chinese are part of the curriculum. Boys and girls are educated separately.

Summer camps are held every year. For information about our schools and summer camp, please visit our website at *www.igdvs.org*

Dharma Realm Buddhist Association
www.drba.org/www.drbachinese.org

Venerable Master Hua's words to children:

Young friends, you are like young trees growing taller day by day, and in the future you will become the pillars of your country. You should do great things and work for world peace.

First, you must learn to be a good person. What is a good person? A good person is respectful to his parents, respectful to his teachers and helpful to his friends and his country. Under the leadership of good people, a nation will be strong, peaceful and prosperous. It is your responsibility is to stop the wars in the world so everyone can be safe and happy, well-fed and well-clothed. Then the world will be in harmony.

Adapted from Talks on Dharma, Volume 9, page 3

Bhikshuni*Jin Rou is the author of many Buddhist books for children, including *The Kind Monk, Under the Bodhi Tree* and a series of Jataka Tales on ecology. She is also editor of *Wok Wisely: Chinese Vegetarian Cooking*.

Terri Nicholson is a teacher and a writer. She is one of the founding teachers of Instilling Goodness School.

Bhikshuni*Heng Ching is a teacher and holds a PhD in Comparative Literature. She has illustrated many books, including *Meditation Handbook, Dew Drops*, and *Snow-Covered Peaks*.

*Bhikshuni is the formal title of an ordained Buddhist nun.

Guan Yin Bodhisattva Album

To hear songs and chanting of Guan Yin's name with Rev. Heng Sure and the Instilling Goodness Choir, visit Dharma Radio. Click on: Guan Yin Bodhisattva Album. www.dharma.radio.org

The Buddha's Helper Parent and Teacher Guide

For a complimentary copy, visit Dharma Radio. Click on: The Buddha's Helper Parent and Teacher Guide. www.dharma.radio.org

www.ingramcontent.com/pod-product-compliance
Lightning Source LLC
LaVergne TN
LVHW072055070426
835508LV00002B/105